TRY NOT TO LAUGH CHALLENGE

CAMPFIRE EDITION

1st edition

ISBN: 9791281216990

CONTACT

TG Edition
Thomas Larch
Ritterweg 16C
39010 St. Martin in Passeier
Italy
E-mail: support@tg-edition.com

IMAGE REFERENCES
freepik

DISCLAIMER

All information, instructions and strategies contained in this book are used at your own risk. The author cannot be held liable for any damages of any kind for any legal reason.

For damages of a material or non-material nature caused by the use or non-use of the information or use of incorrect and/or incomplete information, any liability claims against the author are excluded. Any legal claims and claims for damages are therefore also excluded. This work has been compiled and written down with the utmost care. However, the author does not assume any liability for the topicality, completeness and quality of the information. Misprints and incorrect information cannot be completely ruled out.

No legal responsibility or liability in any form whatsoever can be accepted for incorrect indications.

COPYRIGHT

READY FOR EVEN MORE
CAMPFIRE LAUGHS?

Don't miss your free bonus: 30 hilarious **Would You Rather questions** with a camping twist — perfect for playing around the campfire!

SCAN THE QR CODE

TO DOWNLOAD YOUR FREE CAMPFIRE BONUS RIGHT AWAY!

WELCOME TO THE CAMPFIRE

TRY NOT TO LAUGH CHALLENGE!

HEY THERE, HAPPY CAMPERS!

Get ready for the ultimate laugh battle—perfect for camping trips, cozy nights by the fireplace, or anytime you need a giggle! This book is packed with hilarious camping jokes, from cheesy dad jokes to clever knock-knock jokes and everything in between. Read the jokes to each other and see who can keep a straight face!

HERE'S HOW TO PLAY:

1. **Split into two teams —**
   kids vs. adults works the best!
2. **Take turns reading jokes —**
   one team reads, the other tries not to laugh
3. **Score a point for every laugh you cause**
4. **Play for a few rounds or the whole chapter**
5. **Count the laughs and declare the winner!**

HOW TO KEEP SCORE:

Write down how many points are scored each round. At the end of each chapter, tally up your points and see who scored the most. At the end, see who won the most chapters and crown the Campfire Champions!

TIPS:

- Take turns **reading** the jokes **out loud**
- Use **funny voices** or **silly faces** to deliver your best punchlines
- Play one chapter at a time — or go all in for a full campfire comedy night!
- Most importantly, **HAVE FUN!**

Now grab your team,
warm up your laugh muscles,
& let the showdown begin!

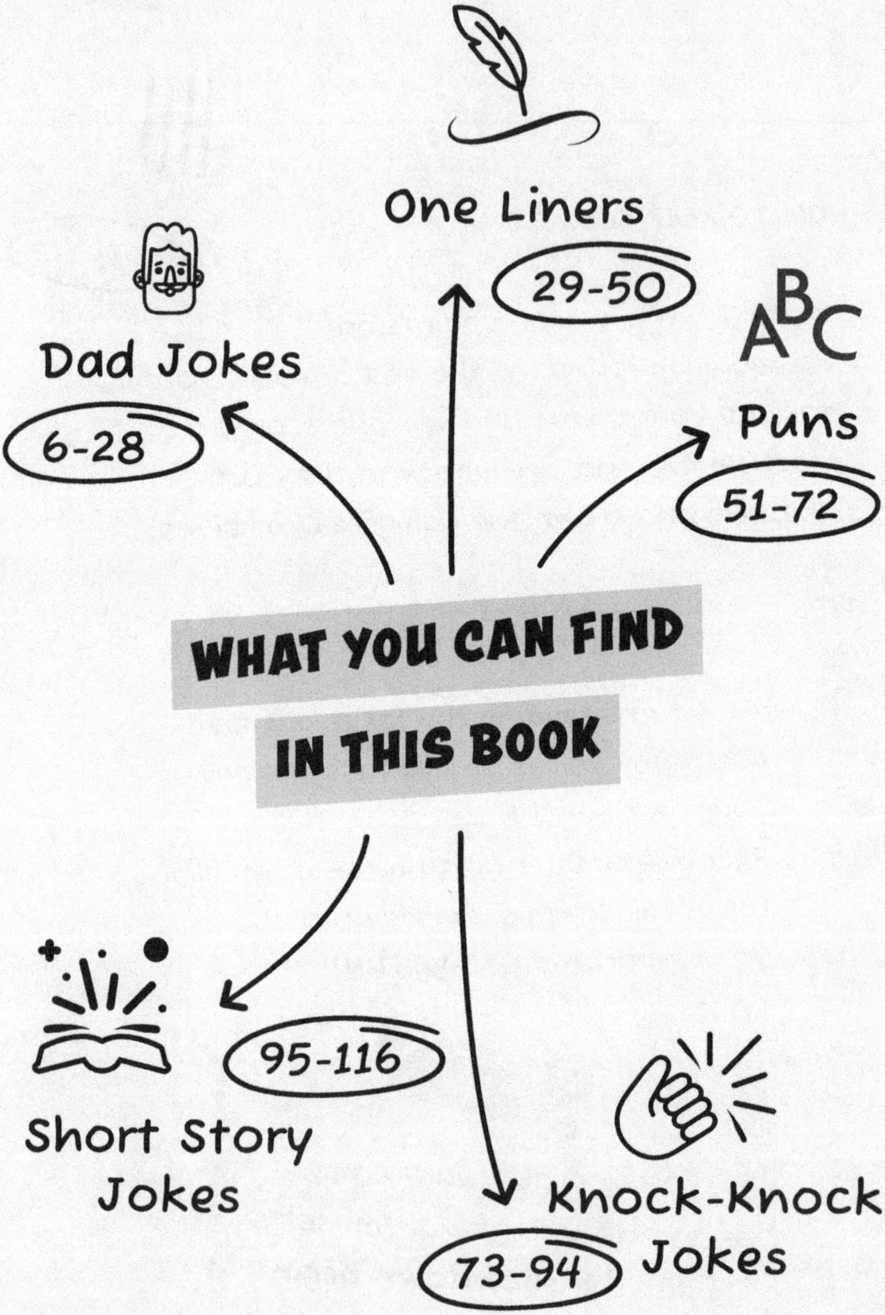

WHAT YOU CAN FIND
IN THIS BOOK
Dad Jokes
6-28
One Liners
29-50
ABC
Puns
51-72
Short Story Jokes
95-116
Knock-Knock Jokes
73-94

DAD JOKES

Get ready for the cheesiest jokes this side of the campfire! These dad-approved groaners are perfect for making your opponents crack up—or cringe.

ROUND 1

TEAM ADULTS

I went to buy a camouflage tent the other day. **I couldn't find any.**

Why did the mushroom go to the camp party?
Because he's a fun guy (fungi).

What do you get when you cross a campfire and a snowman?
A puddle.

Don't trust trees near your campfire;
they can be pretty shady.

Why don't skeletons camp in the forest?
They don't have the guts.

I tried to catch some fog on my hike this morning, but I **mist**.

POINTS

ROUND 1

TEAM KIDS

How do you catch a squirrel at summer camp? **Climb a tree and act like a nut.**

What did one wall say to the other at summer camp? **"I'll meet you at the corner!"**

Can we address the elephant in the tent? **It's a bit cramped in here.**

I got arrested today for putting my arm in a campfire. I got charged with "**having a firearm.**"

Did you hear about the camper that broke his left arm on his last camping trip?
Well, he's all right now.

What do you call a group of grizzly bears telling jokes?
A **bear-rel** of laughs!

POINTS

ROUND 2

TEAM ADULTS

What's a teenager's favorite camping experience? Spending the night in front of **Best Buy for the latest video game.**

What did the beaver say to the tree? It's been nice **gnawing** you.

An adventurer lit a fire in his boat while paddling in winter. **He realized you can't have your kayak and heat it, too.**

You can't run through a campsite. You can only ran... **because ran is past tents.**

Did you hear about the bees who fell in love camping? It was **tent to be.**

What do you call a camper driving through frozen rain? **Van Hailin'.**

POINTS

ROUND 2
TEAM KIDS

How do trees access the Internet? **They log in.**

How do you talk to a fish? **Drop it a line.**

What's another name for a sleeping bag? **A nap sack.**

Why are April 1 campers always tired? **They just finished a 31-day March.**

Why do trees have so many friends? **They branch out.**

Why didn't the elephant carry a suitcase camping? **He already had a trunk.**

POINTS

ROUND 3

TEAM ADULTS

Why don't mummies camp? They're afraid to **relax** and **unwind**.

What do you call a bear with no teeth? **A gummy bear.**

What did the camper say after a scary story? **"I can come up with s'more if you'd like."**

Did you hear about the happy camper? Nope, but I heard about **the Jolly Rancher**!

At the campsite, what did the lake say to the sailboat? Nothing, it just **waved**.

POINTS

What's brown, sticky, and found at a camp? **A stick**.

ROUND 3

TEAM KIDS

What do you call an emergency shelter from cereal boxes?
A snap, crackle, and pop-up tent.

What did the pine trees wear to the lake? **Swim trunks.**

What do you call a camper without a face or body?

Why did the banana go to the camp doctor? Because it wasn't **peeling well!**

Where does a camper keep his money? In the **River Bank**.

How can you identify a dogwood tree? **By its bark**.

POINTS

ROUND 4

TEAM ADULTS

Why did the fish blush? Because it saw the **lake's bottom.**

What camping spot makes a bird sing? **The Canary Islands.**

What's a tree's favorite drink? **Root beer.**

Where do sheep
like to camp?
The Baa-hamas.

Why did the robot go camping?
He needed to **recharge his batteries.**

Why does Humpty Dumpty
like autumn camping? Because he
had **a great fall.**

POINTS

ROUND 4

TEAM KIDS

Why are hiking shops diverse?
They employ people from all walks of life.

Why did the park ranger quit?
Because it was **too in-tents.**

Did you hear about the skunk who went camping? Probably for the best... **it really stinks.**

Why didn't the bike want to camp? It was **two tired.**

Give a man a **fish**, feed him for **a day**. Teach him **to fish**, get rid of him **for a weekend.**

Did you hear about the kidnapping in the woods? It's alright. **He woke up.**

POINTS

ROUND 5

TEAM ADULTS

If RV campers have no lawn decorations, what do they have? **Mobile gnomes.**

Why are RV campers obedient? They go where they're **towed.**

How would you describe a happy camper? **Con-tent.**

Why is tuna perfect for dolphins and campers? Good for all **in-tents and porpoises.**

Get cold camping? Stand in the tent corner. It's usually **90 degrees.**

What's a mosquito's favorite sport? **Skin diving.**

POINTS

ROUND 5

TEAM KIDS

My kids think my geology jokes are lame. I think they **rock.**

God gave us shin bones to find **trailer hitches in the dark.**

Where do cows go camping? **Upstate Moo York.**

Relax! You're **too tents.**

I'm on a
seafood diet.
I see food,
and I eat it.

What vegetables like
to camp?
Brussel scouts.

POINTS

TEAM ADULTS	TEAM KIDS

02

ONE LINERS

Quick, snappy laughs are coming your way! Fire off these zingers around the campfire to catch your opponents off guard.

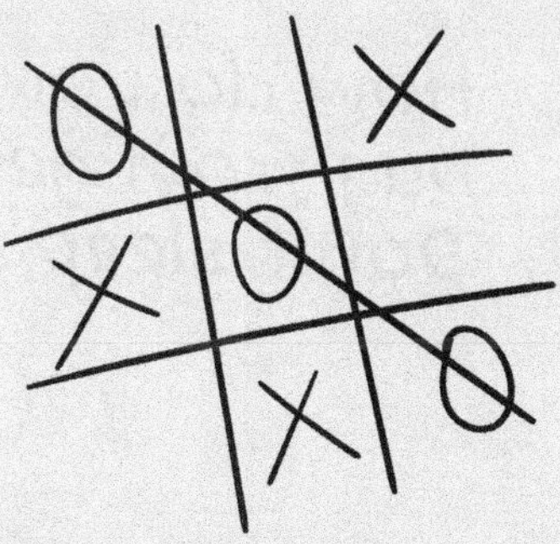

ROUND 1

TEAM ADULTS

What do you call a bunch of crows out for camping? **Murder within tent.**

What did the bears say when they saw tourists in sleeping bags? **"Sandwiches!"**

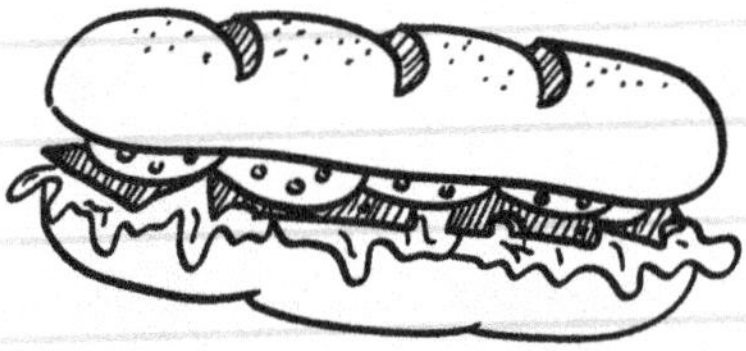

How do you keep your sleeping bag from getting stretched out? **Don't sleep too long in it.**

Why don't eggs tell jokes?
They'd crack each other up.

The seaside camping trip was so boring that **the tide went out one day** and **never returned.**

I slept like a log last night.
I woke up on the campfire.

POINTS

ROUND 1

TEAM KIDS

What day is best for beach camping? **Sun-day.**

Why did the camper bring a pen to the campfire? **To draw closer to the flames.**

What kind of tree fits in your hand? **A palm tree!**

How do you organize a space camp? **You planet.**

Why do campfires tell stories? Because they like to be **the center of the heat.**

What do you call an alligator in a vest? **An investigator.**

POINTS

ROUND 2

TEAM ADULTS

What do you call a snake that works for the government?
A civil serpent.

Why did the bear go to the doctor?
Because he was feeling **a little grizzly.**

What do you call a deer with no eyes? **No idea.**

What shoes do frogs wear camping in summer?
Open-toad shoes.

Why did the scarecrow win the summer camp award?
Because he was **outstanding in his field!**

What do you call a pile of cats in a tent?
A purr-adise.

POINTS

ROUND 2

TEAM KIDS

What do you have when you have three sleeping bags in one hand and three tents in the other hand? **Really big hands!**

Why do hikers always sleep under the stars? Because it's **5-million-star accommodation!**

Why did the fox go to the gym? To work on his **sly-ceps.**

Why did the cellphone go on vacation? It needed to **charge its batteries!**

What's a frog's favorite music service? **Spot-a-fly!**

What do you call a fish with no eyes? **Fsh.**

POINTS

ROUND 3

TEAM ADULTS

Why did Mom throw butter out of the tent? She wanted to see **a butterfly**!

What do you call a tent with a fly? A **bug hotel**.

Where do ants go camping? **Frants**.

What type of chair is good at yoga? **A folding chair.**

What do you call a pile of bears in a tent? **A bear-adise.**

What do you call a fly with no wings? **A walk.**

POINTS

ROUND 3

TEAM KIDS

What do spiders do at camp? **Fly fishing.**

What did the campers say when the guides asked them how they enjoyed the campfire? They all gave it **glowing reviews.**

What warm drink helps you relax while camping? **Calm-omile tea.**

How do computer programmers make extra money in the summer?
They make a **small fortune helping campers get rid of bugs.**

What do you call a camping trip without bug spray?
A feast for mosquitoes.

What did one marshmallow say to the other at the campfire?
You're on fire!

POINTS

ROUND 4
TEAM ADULTS

What did the tent say to the sleeping bag? Don't worry; **I've got you covered!**

Why was the campfire so popular? **It was lit!**

What did the campfire say to the marshmallow? Don't make me **roast you!**

What's a camper's favorite unit of power? **The watt-erfall!**

I'm reading a book on anti-gravity while camping; **it's impossible to put down!**

Why do mummies like camping so much? **They love to 'wrap' up by the fire!**

POINTS

ROUND 4

TEAM KIDS

What do you call a thief who's gone camping? **Criminal intent.**

Where do sharks like to camp? **Fin-land.**

Where does Dale Earnhardt Jr. camp? **In Mada-nascar.**

What does Barry Allen always bring camping? **A flashlight.**

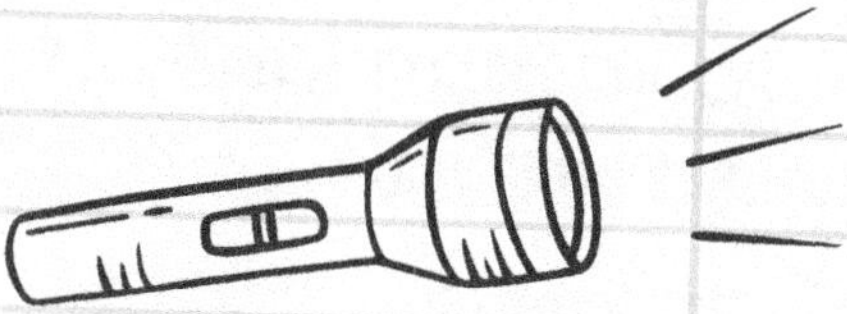

Why don't campfires ever get cold? **They're always too fired up!**

What's green and loves camping?
A boy sprout.

POINTS

ROUND 5

TEAM ADULTS

My wife and I camped to save our marriage. **It was an in-tents situation.**

How do you know if a bear is in your campsite? **You'll see paw-sitive evidence.**

What kind of music do you listen to while camping? **Rock 'n' Roast!**

The deer told me a camping joke, but it was too **fawn-cy**.

What's a camper's worst nightmare? A bear with a **picnic basket**!

What did the tree say to the camper? **Leaf me alone**!

POINTS

ROUND 5

TEAM KIDS

Why don't ants get sick? Because they have **tiny ant-bodies!**

What's a camper's favorite type of math? **Camp-u-lations!**

Why did the firefly get good grades in school? **Because he was bright.**

Why did the math book look sad at camp? Because it had **too many problems**!

Why did the campfire always win arguments? Because it always **had a burning point**.

How do you catch a bear at camp? With your **bear hands**!

POINTS

TEAM ADULTS	TEAM KIDS

PUNS

Pitch your tent and prepare for pun-tastic fun! These gems will have everyone roaring by the campfire.

ROUND 1

TEAM ADULTS

Camping is **in-tents!**

For all in-tents and purposes, camping is just **sleeping outside!**

Me & campfires? **The perfect match!**

ABC

I could go camping **forest of my life!**

How do you learn more about spiders that live in the forest? **Check out their website.**

POINTS

I went for a hike, now I feel **oak-ay.**

ROUND 1

TEAM KIDS

These bad camping puns really **yurt** me.

My team won the **camp-ionship.**

Camping? **Alpaca my tent!**

The campers pitched their tent in the perfect spot; it was **un-tent-ionally** ideal.

The world needs **s'more people** like you.

The campers were so tired after hiking they were **in-tents-ly** exhausted.

POINTS

ROUND 2

TEAM ADULTS

The campfire was so bright, it was **in-tents-ifying.**

The campsite was so calm, it was **tent-ionally** serene.

Loosen up, you're **too tents.**

Wood you please **start a fire?**

We're out of firewood —
don't flame the messenger!

Thank you very match for
starting the fire.

POINTS

ROUND 2

TEAM KIDS

Being around a warm campfire is **pyro-dise**.

The bear wandered into the campground, but it was **un-bear-able**.

Nothing can hold a **kindle** to a **warm campfire**.

All's fire in **love and camping.**

The squirrel that stole their food was **un-bear-ably** sneaky.

The campfire ghost story was so intense it was **fire-tening.**

POINTS

ROUND 3

TEAM ADULTS

You've really got a chip on your **smolder**.

My camping skills are **in-tents-ly** impressive.

The **s'more** the merrier.

ABC

Always be **camp-timistic**.

No more bad camping puns!
I can't bear it!

They roasted marshmallows until they were **marsh-mellowed** out.

POINTS

ROUND 3

TEAM KIDS

S'more fun than you can handle.

Campers have **s'more** fun.

I'm feeling **s'more and s'more** in love with camping.

Laugh **s'more**, worry less.

Camping: like many of the best things in life, it's **tree**.

I **wood** never leaf this place.

POINTS

ROUND 4

TEAM ADULTS

It's all good in the **woods**.

Let's go camping, just for the **hill of it**!

You're invading my personal **spruce**!

ABC

I need my **alone pine.**

I conifer you a discount on **camping puns.**

The campers had a **berry good** time picking wild berries.

POINTS

ABC

ROUND 4

TEAM KIDS

The campers were **berry excited** to go berry picking.

Taking a break from camping to catch **summer rays**.

I can't take my dad camping anymore; he tends to **s'more**.

They couldn't **bear** the thought of leaving the beautiful campsite.

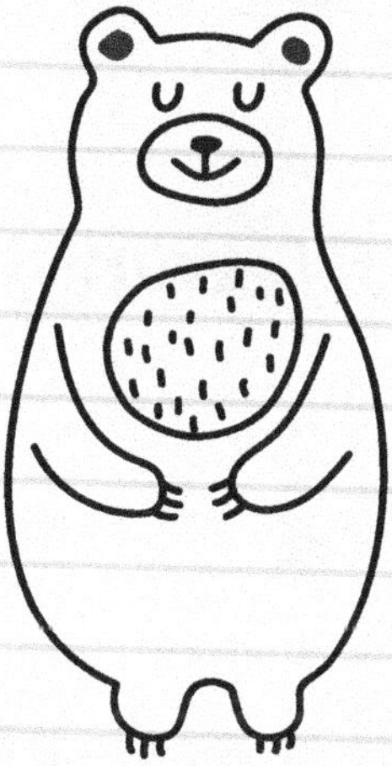

What do you call a bear that's stuck in the rain? **A drizzly bear.**

On my first camping trip, I asked my dad for a **gummy bear.** And he brought me a **grizzly with no teeth!**

POINTS

ROUND 5

TEAM ADULTS

The mosquitoes at the campsite were really **bugging the campers.**

Campers: Nature's way of **feeding mosquitoes.**

You can't **have your kayak** and **eat it too!**

RV there yet?

The campers couldn't bear the cold weather; it was **un-bear-able**.

POINTS

I **caravan** about you.

ROUND 5

TEAM KIDS

Bikes don't often go camping; they're **usually too tired**.

Let's go camping — **try not to s'more**.

I told a **scary story** at the campsite, and now everyone's **in-tent** on leaving!

ABC

This campfire is **lit-erally** the best!

Don't **leaf** me alone in the woods!

The camping trip was intense, but they had a good **in-tent** to stay.

POINTS

TEAM ADULTS	TEAM KIDS

04

KNOCK-KNOCK JOKES

Knock, knock—who's there?
Hilarious camping quips!
Call out these classics to see who can't help but giggle.

ROUND 1

TEAM ADULTS

Knock, knock.
Who's there?
Atch.
Atch who?
Bless you!
Did you catch a cold camping?

Knock, knock!
Who's there?
RV.
RV who?
RV there yet?

Knock, knock!
Who's there?
Moose!
Moose who?
Moose you.
I hope you're having fun away at sleep-away camp!

Knock, knock.
Who's there?
Harry.
Harry who?
Harry up and set up the tent!

Knock, knock.
Who's there?
Noah.
Noah who?
Noah good place to camp around here?

Knock, knock.
Who's there?
Wanda.
Wanda who?
Wanda go camping with me?

POINTS

ROUND 1

TEAM KIDS

Knock, knock.
Who's there?
Al.
Al who?
Al give you a hand with that tent!

Knock, knock.
Who's there?
Ben.
Ben who?
Ben waiting to go camping all year!

Knock, knock.
Who's there?
Sam.
Sam who?
Sam person who loves camping!

Knock, knock.
Who's there?
Shelby.
Shelby who?
Shelby bringing the s'mores?

Knock, knock.
Who's there?
Tent.
Tent who?
Tent-atively planning our epic camping adventure!

Knock, knock.
Who's there?
Earl.
Earl who?
Earl be glad when we get to the campsite!

POINTS

ROUND 2
TEAM ADULTS

Knock, knock.
Who's there?
Gus.
Gus who?
Gus what? We're going camping!

Knock, knock.
Who's there?
Ida.
Ida who?
Ida rather be camping!

Knock, knock.
Who's there?
Will.
Will who?
Will you help me pitch this tent?

Knock, knock.
Who's there?
Hugo.
Hugo who?
Hugo first, I'll follow with the gear!

Knock, knock.
Who's there?
Ivan.
Ivan who?
Ivan to go camping, let's go!

Knock, knock.
Who's there?
Abby.
Abby who?
Abby birthday, let's go camping!

POINTS

ROUND 2

TEAM KIDS

Knock, knock.
Who's there?
Anita.
Anita who?
Anita tent for this camping trip!

Knock, knock.
Who's there?
Dewey.
Dewey who?
Dewey have to sleep in this tent?

Knock, knock.
Who's there?
Isle.
Isla who?
Isle be seeing you at the campfire!

Knock, knock.
Who's there?
Yul.
Yul who?
Yul love camping once you try it!

Knock, knock.
Who's there?
Zee.
Zee who?
Zee you later, I'm going camping!

Knock, knock.
Who's there?
Lettuce.
Lettuce who?
Lettuce go camping!

POINTS

ROUND 3
TEAM ADULTS

Knock, knock.
Who's there?
Andy.
Andy who?
Andy one want to go camping with me?

Knock, knock.
Who's there?
Colin.
Colin who?
Colin all campers, time for fun!

Knock, knock.
Who's there?
Armageddon.
Armageddon who?
Armageddon cold out here!

Knock, knock.
Who's there?
Lettuce.
Lettuce who?
Lettuce in; it's cold outside!

Knock, knock.
Who's there?
Canoe.
Canoe who?
Canoe come out and play with me?

Knock, knock.
Who's there?
Carrie.
Carrie who?
Carrie these camping chairs, please.

POINTS

ROUND 3

TEAM KIDS

Knock, knock.
Who's there?
Hoo.
Who hoo?
Uh oh, watch out for the owl!

Knock, knock.
Who's there?
Hike.
Hike who?
I didn't know you liked hiking, too!

Knock, knock.
Who's there?
Wooden.
Wooden who?
Wooden you like to hear another camping joke?

Knock, knock.
Who's there?
S'more.
S'more who?
S'more camping, please!

Knock, knock.
Who is there?
Ken!
Ken who?
Ken you also hear something growling?

Knock, knock.
Who's there?
Bear.
Bear who?
Bear with me; I've got more camping jokes!

POINTS

ROUND 4

TEAM ADULTS

Knock, knock.
Who is there?
Annie!
Annie who?
Annie more marshmallows to eat on the campfire?

Knock, knock.
Who's there?
Tent.
Tent who?
Tent you hear?
I'm telling jokes!

Knock, knock.
Who's there?
Arh.
Arh who?
Arh you going to tell another joke?

Knock, knock.
Who is there?
Arthur!
Arthur who?
Arthur any spiders at the campsite?

Knock, knock.
Who is there?
Colleen!
Colleen who?
Colleen up the mess at the campsite before you leave.

Knock, knock.
Who is there?
Matt!
Matt who?
Matt-resses at this camp are hard as rocks.

POINTS

ROUND 4
TEAM KIDS

Knock, knock.
Who is there?
Kent!
Kent who?
Kent you please paddle any faster?

Knock, knock.
Who's there?
Fishing.
Fishing who?
Fishing for compliments, how's my camping skills?

Knock, knock.
Who's there?
Otto.
Otto who?
Otto know where the best campsites are!

Knock, knock.
Who's there?
Olive.
Olive who?
Olive camping, how about you?

Knock, knock.
Who's there?
Bear.
Bear who?
Bear-ly sleeping, I'm too excited for camping!

Knock, knock.
Who's there?
Donut.
Donut who?
Donut forget to bring marshmallows for the campfire!

POINTS

ROUND 5

TEAM ADULTS

Knock, knock.
Who's there?
Firewood.
Firewood who?
Firewood like to tell you some campfire jokes!

Knock, knock.
Who's there?
Raccoon.
Raccoon who?
Rac-coon't wait to explore the great outdoors with you!

Knock, knock.
Who's there?
Hiking.
Hiking who?
Hiking all day, camping all night, that's the way to do it right!

Knock, knock.
Who's there?
A little old lady.
A little old lady who?
I didn't know you could yodel, I'll join you for camping trip!

Knock, knock.
Who's there?
Boo.
Boo who?
Don't cry, it's just a camping trip!

Knock, knock.
Who's there?
Woody.
Woody who?
Woody like to go camping with me?

POINTS

ROUND 5

TEAM KIDS

Knock, knock.
Who's there?
Justin.
Justin who?
Justin time for the campfire!

Knock, knock.
Who's there?
Luke.
Luke who?
Luke out, there's a bear!

Knock, knock.
Who's there?
Howard.
Howard who?
Howard you like to sleep in a tent?

Knock, knock.
Who's there?
Peas.
Peas who?
Peas pass the marshmallows!

Knock, knock.
Who's there?
Orange.
Orange who?
Orange you glad we're camping?

Knock, knock.
Who's there?
Dishes.
Dishes who?
Dishes a great place to camp!

POINTS

TEAM ADULTS	TEAM KIDS

05

Short Story Jokes

Gather 'round for tales with a twist! These mini campfire story jokes are your secret weapon to stump the other team.

ROUND 1
TEAM ADULTS

Deer-ly Departed

Two deer hunters hired a pilot to take them way back into the forest. After the hunt, the pilot returned and saw that they had six deer. "The plane won't carry six deer; you'll have to leave two of them," said the pilot. Unwilling to leave their deer, the hunters said, "We got six on the plane last year." After going back and forth for a few minutes, the pilot gave in, and just five minutes after takeoff, the plane crashed into the forest. Lucky to be alive, one of the hunters said, "Any idea where we are?" The second hunter said, "Yeah, right about where our plane went down last year."

Lost in the Wilderness

A man got lost on a camping trip. Rescuers scoured the wilderness until a medical emergency team finally spotted a solitary figure across a wide chasm. "Charlie Smith," someone shouted, "is that you?" "Yes, it is," came the reply. "Who are you?" "We're from the Red Cross." "I gave at the office!" Charlie shouted back.

POINTS

ROUND 1
TEAM KIDS

What's Bugging You?

While sitting around a campfire, a boy asks his father, "Dad, are bugs good to eat?" "That's disgusting. Don't talk about things like that over dinner," the dad replies. After dinner, the father asks, "Now, son, what did you want to ask me?" "Oh, nothing," the boy says. "There was a bug in your soup, but now it's gone."

Camping with Bears

A man takes along a bat to go camping. His friend asks if it's for the bears. Man: "No. This will not stop a bear." Friend: "What will you do if a bear crosses our path?" Man: "I'll run." Friend: "Run? You can't outrun a bear."
Man: "I don't have to. I just have to outrun you." Friend: "But you can't outrun me." Man: "That's what the bat is for."

POINTS

ROUND 2
TEAM ADULTS

LA Late-Night Bear Encounter

I went on a camping trip with my wife, kids, and mother-in-law. At night, my wife awoke to find her mother gone. Rushing to me, she insisted on trying to find her mother. I picked up my rifle, took a swig of whiskey, and started to look for her. In a clearing not far from the camp, we came upon a chilling sight. The mother-in-law was backed up against a thick, impenetrable bush, and a large bear stood facing her. My wife cried, "What are we going to do?" "Nothing," I said. "The bear got himself into this mess; let him get himself out of it."

A Ringing End

A hiker goes into a store and asks about bears in the area. The store owner explained that there were black bears and grizzlies, and to avoid surprising them, hikers should wear bear bells. The hiker buys a couple of bells and then asks how to tell the difference between black bear and grizzly scat. The owner says, "Black bear scat is smaller and has berries and squirrel fur. Grizzly scat has bells in it."

POINTS

ROUND 2

TEAM KIDS

Bathroom Breaks

A young boy goes camping in the woods for the first time with his dad. After they set up camp, he asks his dad where he can go to the toilet. "That's the beauty of camping in the woods," the father replies, "You can go to the toilet wherever you want." After five minutes or so, the young lad wanders back to the campfire. "So, where did you go to the toilet then, son?" The father asks. "In your tent," the boy replies.

Perfect Match

"My son and I went camping yesterday, and he asked me how to start a campfire. I explained, "You can start a fire by rubbing two sticks together, but make sure they're the same. Then you'll have a match."

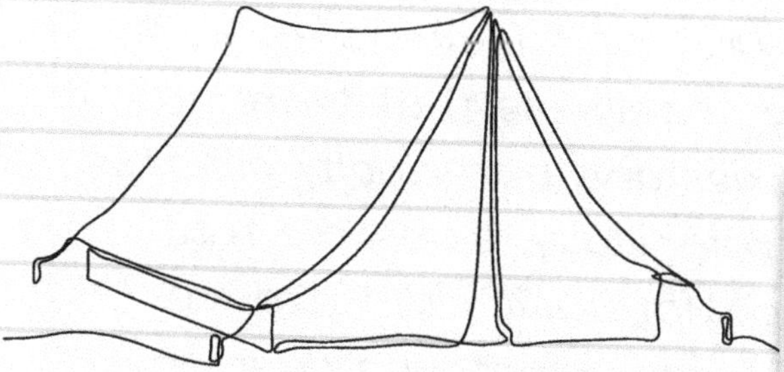

POINTS

ROUND 3
TEAM ADULTS

A Night Under the Stars

Sherlock Holmes and Dr Watson go on a camping trip together. After eating their dinner around the campfire, they retire to the tent to go to sleep. A few hours later, Sherlock wakes up. "Watson, are you awake?" He asks. "Yes, sir. What is it?" Answers Watson. "Look up and tell me what you see." Asks Holmes. "I see billions of stars," says Watson. "And what does that tell you, Watson," asks Holmes. "Well," says Dr Watson, "Astronomically, it tells me that there are millions of galaxies and potentially billions of planets. Astrologically, I observe that Saturn is in Leo. Horologically, I deduce that the time is approximately a quarter past three. Theologically, I can see that God is all-powerful and that we are small and insignificant. Meteorologically, I suspect that we will have a beautiful day tomorrow." "Why? – What does it tell you, Holmes?" Holmes is quiet for a moment, then says: "It tells me that someone has stolen our tent."

POINTS

ROUND 3

TEAM KIDS

Don't Forget to Write It Down

There was an elderly couple who, in their old age, noticed that they were getting a lot more forgetful, so they decided to go to the doctor. The doctor told them they should start writing things down so they don't forget. A couple days later, they went camping, and the old lady told her husband to make her a cup of coffee. "You might want to write it down," she said. The husband said, "No, I can remember that you want a cup of coffee." She then told her husband she wanted a cup of coffee with cream. "Write it down," she told him, and again, he said, "No, no, I can remember: you want a cup of coffee with cream." Then, the old lady said she wanted a cup of coffee with cream and sugar. "Write it down," she told her husband, and again he said, "No, I got it. You want a cup of coffee with cream and sugar." So he goes to get the coffee and spends an unusually long time outside of the tent, over 30 minutes. He returns to his wife and hands her a plate of eggs and bacon. The old wife stares at the plate for a moment, then looks at her husband and asks, "Where's the toast?"

POINTS

ROUND 4
TEAM ADULTS

Say It Slow...

A husband and wife were driving through the mountains. As they approached their campsite, they started arguing about the pronunciation of the town. They continued to argue back and forth as they stopped for lunch. At the counter, the husband asked the blonde waitress, "Before we order, could you please settle an argument for us? Would you please pronounce where we are very slowly?" She leaned over the counter and said, "Burrr-gerrr Kiiing."

What's in a Name?

A child goes to his father and asks, "Father, how do parents think of names for their children?" The father answers, "Well, son, the night before the mother gives birth, the father goes into the woods and camps for the night. When he wakes the following morning, the first thing he sees is what he names his child, which is why your sister is named Soaring Eagle. Why do you ask, Bear Poop?"

POINTS

ROUND 4
TEAM KIDS

Amen, Bear!

Two guys are walking through a national park and come across a bear that has not eaten for days. The bear sees the two men and starts chasing them. They run as fast as they can, and one guy starts getting tired and decides to say a prayer, "Please turn this bear into a Christian, Lord." He looks to see if the bear is still chasing, and he sees the bear on its knees. Happy to see his prayer answered, he turns around and heads towards the bear. As he approaches the bear, he hears it saying a prayer: "Thank you, Lord, for the food I am about to receive."

The Sofa Survivalist

"My wife was surprised to hear that I actually enjoyed her punishment of making me sleep on the sofa. I said that it made me feel manly like I was camping. With a really angry bear somewhere close by..."

POINTS

ROUND 5
TEAM ADULTS

Wrong Target

A man walks out of his tent one day and sees a fox in the tree in front of his campsite. Unsure of what to do, he calls animal control. About an hour later, a man shows up with a ladder, a pit bull, and a taser. The animal control employee tells the man, "I'm here to get the fox out of your tree. I'm going to use this ladder to climb up the tree and shake the branch the fox is on to knock him to the ground. The pit bull is trained to attack anything that falls from the tree." The man says, "Okay, I see what the ladder and the pit bull are for, but what is the taser for?" The animal control employee says, "Oh, that's for you. In case I fall out of the tree instead of the fox, shoot the dog."

Spin Cycle: River Edition

A young camper is swimming in a river. A man walks up and asks him, "What are you doing in there?" He says, "I'm washing my clothes." The man asks, "Why don't you use a washing machine?" The camper says, "I tried that, but I got too dizzy."

Bald on Bald

The sight of a bald eagle has thrilled campers for generations. However, the sight of a bald man does absolutely nothing for the eagle.

POINTS

ROUND 5
TEAM KIDS

Ruff Prices

A dog goes into a camping store and buys a tent. The cashier says, "You don't see a dog in here buying a tent very often." The dog says, "At these prices, I'm not surprised."

Track Trouble

Three campers were walking in the woods and came upon tracks. The first one said, "Look, it's deer tracks." The second one said, "No, it's wolf tracks." Before the third one could answer, they got hit by a train.

The Spider Situation

A spider was in my tent, and my girlfriend told me to take it out instead of squashing it. We went and had some drinks. Cool guy. Wants to be a lawyer.

POINTS

TEAM ADULTS	TEAM KIDS

AND THE FINAL WINNER IS...

	TEAM ADULTS	TEAM KIDS
1. ROUND		
2. ROUND		
3. ROUND		
4. ROUND		
5. ROUND		
FINAL POINTS		

AFTERWORD

Thanks for joining the **Campfire Joke Showdown** — we hope you laughed and giggled your way through every round!

Whether you played around a real campfire, at home, or just shared a few jokes with a friend, remember: **the best laughs are the ones we share together.** Keep telling jokes, keep making memories, and don't forget — the next laugh battle is always just one punchline away.

Until next time...

... Stay silly & keep **the campfire spirit alive!**

THANK YOU FOR YOUR PURCHASE!

We hope you enjoyed the Book.
If you liked the book, please leave a review on Amazon.
Thank you!

EXPLORE THE FULL SERIES:

SCAN HERE

TO DISCOVER OUR JOKE BOOK SERIES

Made in United States
North Haven, CT
27 July 2025

71075054R00065